THE TRUE STORY
OF THE
LOCH
NESS
MONSTER

Also by
FRANCES GILBERT

FOR CHILDREN

Turtle On A Summer's Day
Celeste and Regine In The Rainforest
A World Of Numbers
To Know The Sea
Goodnight World Outside
Elephant Blue
The Cookie Thief
Today the Teacher Changed Our Seats
The Man With A Pocketful Of Bees

SHORT FICTION FOR ADULTS

Where Is She Now?
She Should Have Come For Me
Village Dream

THE TRUE STORY
OF THE
LOCH NESS MONSTER

FRANCES GILBERT

illustrations by Rhett Pennell

FRANCES GILBERT BOOKS

Dedication

In memory of
Mustuni,
cat of distinction.

Illustrations and Book Design by Rhett Pennell

Published by Frances Gilbert Books
www.francesgilbert.com

First Edition 2017

If you want to know the true story of the Loch Ness Monster you must climb the hills above Drumnadrochit and look for a wee white cottage. In it lives an old lady and she will tell you the truth of it, but she is very old now and her mind wanders, so whether you believe her or not is up to you! As she would say, "People believe what they want to believe, see what they want to see."

Anyway I went to see her one day and this is what she told me.

Many years ago she was living in that cottage with her two young sons Davey and Hamish, and fine strong wee boys they were too, and grew up to be fine strong young men, for didn't she give them a good nourishing rice pudding breakfast every day, with cinnamon and raisins in and didn't they eat every bit of it?

By and by these strapping young men got so big that they knocked everything about when they came in from the hills and threw off their jackets; their muddy boots filled up the porch; wet hats and gloves dripped all over the range in the kitchen and jumpers and socks were all over the floor in their bedroom, and their little old mother tripped and stumbled about the house until one day she said,

"That's it! You are big enough now to go out into the world and seek your fortunes." Then Davey said at once that he would go to sunny Australia to be a veterinarian and Hamish said he would go to Patagonia in sunny South America to be a sheep farmer, and the old lady said that would be a fine plan and they were to be sure to write to tell her all their adventures and to meet good Scots lasses to be their wives. So it was decided, and the old lady washed their jumpers and socks one last time, sewed up all the pockets on their jackets, replaced the missing buttons and hung out their kilts to air.

"It's a fine opportunity they are having, away out of the rains," she said to herself, "I'm glad for them, and I won't think now about how I'll miss them."

Davey and Hamish went off to the pub in the village on their last night at home. They drank a toast to sunny Australia and sunny South America and then clinked their glasses again and drank to sunny South America and sunny Australia, but then they grew sad at the thought of leaving their dear little mother, and first Davey, then Hamish, began to weep into their drinks.

"We canna go," sobbed Davey, "who will she feed with the rice pudding every morning?"

"Aye," hiccupped Hamish, "and who will cuddle with her in the chair by the fire to watch the telly?"

And they both had another drink to toast their dear mother and wept some more.

An old man had been sitting at the bar listening to them.

"Whisht laddies," he said, "it's a fine opportunity you have ahead of you in sunny Australia and sunny South America, away out of the rains. Dinna turn it down. What your mother needs is a wee companion, and I have the very one right here."

He reached into his bulging pocket and pulled out a tangle of kittens and put them on the counter. The kittens scrambled about licking up the puddles and stealing crisps. One wee black fellow hung himself upside down over the edge of the bar and clawed at Davey's sleeve. Davey plucked him up and the kitten climbed up his jumper, purring as loud as a tractor and tangling its claws in his beard.

"Och, that's it," cried Hamish," won't she be giving him the rice pudding now and won't he be cuddling with her in the chair by the fire to watch the telly?"

"That'll be a pound," said the old man and then they had another drink to toast the kitten and another to toast the old man and all in all it was quite late by the time Davey and Hamish said good-bye and set off up the hill to the cottage. Davey tried to carry the kitten in his cap but he wouldn't stay put and hung himself upside down out of the cap, and then he dragged himself up his jacket and dug his claws into Davey's neck

"Och, the wee monster," he said.

"Give him here," said Hamish and he took off his boot and put the kitten down inside and carried him home that way. He didn't mind about his wet foot; most of the time his feet were wet anyway.

Their mother was waiting up for them and she looked cross when she saw Hamish with only one boot on, but Davey quickly said, "Look, we brought you a wee companion so you won't be lonely when we're gone."

"Yes, said Hamish, "a wee fella for you to talk to when you're on your own."

He put his boot on the ground and the kitten came out and pawed about the doorstep with his tail in the air.

"Och, the wee fella," said the old lady, "he'll be a fine companion I'm sure. Now come on in and have the last of the rice pudding before you're away in the morning."

The kitten clung on to the edge of the old lady's skirt and swung himself up the doorstep, wobbled into the kitchen, and set about chasing the hens out from the cupboard under the sink. Then he pummeled a pile of dusters until he had made himself a bed and went to sleep, purring like a tractor.

"Would you look at him now," said the

old lady, "he's quite at home."

Then Davey and Hamish felt a lot better about leaving their little mother to go to sunny Australia and sunny South America.

When the old lady came downstairs in the morning Davey and Hamish were gone, the hens were back in the cupboard under the sink, and the kitten was sitting up in Hamish's place at the table, with Hamish's blue napkin round his neck, waiting for his breakfast.

"Would you look at that, the wee monster!" said the old lady delightedly, and she quickly made a new batch of rice pudding with plenty of raisins and cinnamon and she and the kitten ate breakfast together.

The old lady was very pleased with her new companion. Every morning they had the rice pudding together, then the old lady washed the dishes while the kitten chased the hens outside and scrambled up the curtains to whisk his tail at the spiders until they ran back into their cracks in the wall. In the afternoons the old lady worked in her garden digging potatoes and the kitten stalked about and pounced on her boots. In the evenings they watched telly together in the chair by the fire.

By and by the old lady began to realize that she was making enormous amounts of rice pudding every day and the kitten was getting strong and sturdy and very big. Now, when he chased the spiders he brought the curtain poles down and when he scattered the hens he squashed them and he and the old lady had to have quite a few chicken dinners. He had quite outgrown the cupboard under the sink and was sleeping in Davey's bed in the attic, and he had his own chair in the evening to watch the telly.

"Tsk, Tsk," said the old lady, "you're getting to be quite the monster, it's outside for you from now on, away and play on the hills."

So the cat, for that's what he now was, took himself off across the fields, scattering the sheep, and down the hills to the loch side to play. It was tourist season and the cat had a fine time dodging cars, pouncing on cyclists, and rolling the bins in the parking lots into the loch with a great splash and swimming after them.

"Did you see that?" said the tourists, "What ever was it?"

But the cat streaked away into the trees before they could get their cameras ready.

Every morning he would turn up at the old lady's house for his rice pudding and tell her all the news he had heard.

"They are saying there's been sightings of the monster."

"Whisht," said the old lady, "tourists have no sense, they see what they want to see."

The cat liked the nights of the full moon best, when he prowled by the banks of the loch and he and the moon played games with his shadow. He stalked his black shape, and raced after it, stretching himself out long and lean, until the moon took his shadow and threw it on to the loch and he rushed to pounce on it and make it ripple across the water. Then the tourists parked in their motor homes, heard the splashing and glanced out of their windows just in time to see that sinuous shadow die away under the waves.

"It's the monster," they exclaimed and rushed for their cameras, but all they caught was an indistinct black shape by the water's edge.

By and by the rumor grew, The Loch Ness Monster was to be seen on certain nights Drumnadrochit way, and children begged their parents to stop by the loch so they could watch for themselves.

"Foolishness," said the old lady, when she came down to the shop for more rice, "There's nae monster out there, some folks see what they want to see, and believe what they want to believe."

"It's good for business anyway," said the shop keeper.

Eventually the cat grew tired of splashing about along the loch. He was a fine, strapping young cat now, and he wanted to be off adventuring, so he took himself to where the boats were tied up for the night and stowed himself away under a rubber dinghy on one of the bigger sailing boats and the next day set off on a journey up through the locks at Fort Augustus and down the canal through Loch Oich and Loch Lochy to Fort William.

At Fort William he got off and began exploring the banks of Loch Linnhe. He came upon an old gentleman in a rubber suit swimming to and fro just below the Corran ferry.

"That looks fun," he said, "I like to swim, but I can't get very far at all. I really would like

to be able to get up to Fort Augustus now and then for the fish and chips."

"You look pretty strong to me," said the old man, who was a very polite old gentleman and didn't for one minute acknowledge that it was strange to be talking to a cat, "but swimming is all in the kick, you really need the kick."

"The kick is it?" said the cat and he hopped in beside the old man and they practiced all afternoon, but the cat couldn't quite get the kick, and he got discouraged.

"I'm not getting this right." he said, "I'll never manage Drumnadrochit to Fort Augustus in an evening for the fish and chips."

"What you need," said the old man, "is flippers like mine, then you'd have the kick, and the power to go up and down the loch."

The cat thanked the old man for his advice and hopped aboard a fishing boat for the return journey. He crouched under a piece of sacking and thought about flippers.

When the boat reached Fort Augustus the fishermen tied up at the top of the locks and went off for their suppers. There was a fine smell of fish and chips and the cat licked his whiskers, he hadn't had his rice pudding for a few days and he was hungry. Boats were tying up all around him waiting for the lock gates to open. A family had just got off the next boat and left an untidy heap of slickers and flippers on deck.

"Just the thing," said the cat, and he

helped himself to a pair of flippers and a yellow slicker. He put the slicker on right away and went to join the queue in the chip shop. When he got up to the counter he was able to snatch up a good hot packet of chips with curry sauce while its owner was searching in his pockets for his money. He ate his dinner on the boat,

"Not much fish about it," he said to himself, then he put on the flippers and practiced his leg kicks under the spare sail until he heard the crew returning. Leaving his slicker under the sail, he stepped off the boat and while the men were busy with the ropes and everyone's attention was on the boats, for it's a great sight to see the boats come down the locks and there is often quite a bit of excited shouting and swearing and always the possibility of seeing someone fall in, he walked off down the lock steps and across the bridge to the Loch Ness side. He left the slicker on the dock, tightened the straps on his flippers and launched himself into the loch and set out for Drumnadrochit.

Straight away he noticed the difference. It was just as the old man had said; now he had the power with the kick and he was getting up a fine speed. He put his face in the water and the little waves sleeked back his ears; he arched his back and thrust out with his front paws and the flippers kicked him forward in great style. Now

and then he put his head up and admired the long wake he left as he churned on up the lock. When the moon came out she saw him and shone down on his wake so it spread behind him like a great silvery tail, then she dragged the silhouette of his sleek head and threw it in front of him and he and she played dip and drop with his shadow as he powered up the lake fancying himself the very Michael Phelps of felines.

On the shore those tourists who had not gone to bed and who were watching up the loch saw the strange churnings in the water and the silvery wake. They rushed for their binoculars and cameras and some of them managed to get some hasty pictures of a blurred head and what might be the elongated body of a creature making its way up Loch Ness. They sent the pictures to their friends and the next morning there were headlines in the papers 'Loch Ness Monster New Sighting'.

Meanwhile the cat had reached Drum-nadrochit, it took him a very long time and he was very tired, but quite pleased with himself. He slapped home in his flippers and hid them in the hen house, and went inside to tell the old lady of his adventures, although he didn't tell her about the borrowed flippers, of course, because he knew she would be very cross, and anyway he said to himself, 'I will put them back when I'm done with them.'

All that summer the cat swam up the loch twice a week for his fish and chips, and he grew stronger and stronger and his kick more and more powerful until in the end he could manage the journey in forty minutes. He always timed his visits for the lock closings when there were boats tied up and a slicker or a rain jacket left on deck for him to borrow. He always stood quietly in the queue at the fish and chip shop and when a big order was given and put up he quickly helped himself and went off to sit by the locks to eat them. There was such a bustle every day now at Fort Augustus with people coming from all over to see if they could spot the monster, that no one paid any attention to a fine big cat quietly eating his fish and chips. And if you are thinking that it wasn't at honest for the cat to be helping himself to fish and chips without paying for them, all I can say is he was only a cat and he didn't understand about money; many years later when he had become very famous indeed and did understand, he reimbursed the entire cost of the fish and chips to the chip shop in dollars and as the exchange rate was very good at the time they made out very well.

The sightings continued. News teams and television crews rushed up to Inverness and hired boats to patrol the loch for sightings of the monster. They took rooms wherever they could and interviewed anyone and every one. Oh, it was a great excitement! Hotels and bed and breakfasts were booked up, and boats patrolled the loch day and night with searchlights and cameras and clever devices for listening under water. The cat was quite annoyed, there was entirely too much commotion on Loch Ness for his liking, so some nights after his fish and chips he continued up the steps, slid into the canal and set off for Loch Oich. There it was much calmer and under the walls of Invergarry Castle he and the moon played their games.

One night he met the old gentleman again, swimming to and fro in his rubber suit.

"That was good advice you gave me," said the cat, "with these flippers I can really get going. I do Drumnadrochit to Fort Augustus in forty minutes now."

The old man was very impressed, he watched the cat swim and admired his power and gave him some tips on how to improve his breathing and how to swim under water. They practiced together, then they rested on the bank and the old gentleman told the cat tales of the swims he had swum in sunny South Africa, and the places he had been, the adventures he had had.

"It's a great world out there," he said, "and a fine, strong young fella like you should take the chance and go seek your fortune."

"I will indeed," said the cat, "for it's getting entirely too crowded around Fort Augustus way for my liking."

"Good luck," said the old gentleman.

They shook hands and the cat set off to swim back to Drumnadrochit. At Fort Augustus he climbed out of the canal and walked down the lock steps, across the road to the Loch Ness side. He tightened the straps on his flippers and slid into the loch. He swam under water leaving only a slender moon lit trail on the surface, until he was well out into the middle of the loch. Then he arched his back, thrust forward with his paws and powered with the kick. The moon lobbed his shadow ahead of him and he raced after it.   Now and then he put up his sleek head to look back at his wake. The waves behind him, edged by the moon's silvery touch, lapped together and rolled over like the coils of a serpent. Someone in a boat tied up at Foyer's Falls caught the picture on his camera; it was one of the better ones and later in life the cat was very proud of it, 'Didn't I have the style?' he would say.

At Drumnadrochit the cat pulled out of the water and set off for home. He stopped off in the pub for a wee dram. The whole place was buzzing with the story of 'the sightings'.

Reporters were yelling into their phones and interviewing villagers. The cat snatched up a cap that had been left on a chair and pushed up nearer the bar. He helped himself to a spare dram and listened as stories of monsters and sightings of unusual beasts in strange and far-away places were told.

"Och," he said to a reporter, who thrust a microphone into his face, "it's a great world out there right enough, monsters and all, and I'm away tomorrow to seek my own fortune."

Then he excused himself and went off up the hill to the old lady. He told her all about the excitement in the village and the further sightings and the people coming from all over to see the monster.

"Foolishness!" said the old lady, "People see what they want to see and believe what they want to believe, still there is nae doot it's good for the business."

"Aye," said the cat, "It's a mystery right enough, but who knows what's out there!" and he twirled his whiskers and winked at the old lady.

"Get away with you, you big monster!" she said

Loch Ness, twenty miles

long, forms part of the historic Caledonian Canal Waterway which cuts across Scotland, from Inverness to Fort William, a total distance of sixty miles .

Following the canal down to Loch Linnhe by boat, the interested reader can recreate the cat's journey. They may not come across the old lady or the old gentleman in the rubber suit, but everything else is the same.

On nights of the full moon, beautiful and mysterious Loch Ness still fascinates. Who knows what is out there?

- FG

Frances Gilbert was born in Greenwich, UK and spent a war time childhood in Liverpool and London. She emigrated to the United States with her family in the sixties. Frances spent many years as a special education teacher, allowing her to indulge in her love for language and literacy. Encouraged by her daughter Sarah, also a writer, Frances began creating children's stories and psychological mysteries for adults. She writes from her home in Connecticut and retreats to her cottage in the Scottish Highlands for inspiration.

For more information go to *www.francesgilbert.com* and Frances Gilbert Books on Facebook

Printed in Great Britain
by Amazon